Dearest Shweta,

You can do this, th

for love when you lea

UNBLOCK YOUR WOMB

With the 5 Steps Healing Technique

Improve Your Fertility Naturally

VICKI RENZ

Copyright and Disclaimer Info

Published by Victoria Renz, vicki@ohmymamabody.com

2nd Edition - September 2023

Cover Art by: ShiShi Nguyen
Design by: www.bookclaw.com

Disclaimer:

The Reader is solely responsible for creating and implementing the Reader's own physical, mental and emotional well-being. The author is neither liable nor responsible for any actions or inaction for any direct or indirect result of the information provided in this book. The Reader understands the guidance in this book is not therapy and does not substitute treatment if needed. The information given in this book should not be treated as a substitute for medical advice; always consult a medical practitioner.

The author makes no guarantees of the results you'll achieve by reading this book. All healing requires dedication and consistency. The results and client case studies presented in this book represent results achieved working directly with the author. Your results may vary when undertaking self-guided womb healing.

Dedicated to my mother Rosalyn whose struggles showed me to fully trust in my calling to womb healing.
Thank you for your continued love, support and guidance in spirit.

CONTENTS

INTRO - HOW TO READ THIS BOOK

I have written this book for two reasons:

Reason One: To get womb healing understood and accessible to as many women as possible worldwide with well-founded information as to why it works.

Reason Two: To get you results by giving you practical exercises to follow so that you begin to shift blockages from your womb.

I want to help you to heal your fertility struggles so that you regain your quality of life.

To do that, I've structured this book as follows:

Firstly, I would like you to get a good picture of where you currently stand in terms of your womb connection. That way I can give you specific guidance and advice for your best way forward to make progress with your womb healing. You will be completing several self-assessment exercises that will help you to know how best to proceed.

Secondly, it is essential for you to understand how womb healing works and how modern society has led us to become so disconnected from our wombs. We take a look at the struggles so many of us face and I give you tips and techniques to support you to overcome these.

After that I share with you the Five Steps to Womb Healing technique with practical exercises to enable you to learn how to carry out womb healing on yourself.

The goal is for you to be able to begin experiencing an initial shift in your womb blockages by the time you finish reading this book.

The technique you are about to discover radically transformed my own life with positive benefits on so many layers and levels. I reclaimed much more than my fertility; I fell back in love with life.

I sincerely hope you will be able to achieve such uplifting and life changing transformations for yourself as well.

I believe that the number of women struggling with blockages in their womb can be greatly decreased by communicating the knowledge of womb connection through easy to follow steps.

It is a great privilege to share what I know with you. I hope it inspires you to implement the Five Steps Technique consistently on yourself so that you can shift your womb blockages naturally and improve your quality of life.

If you read this book and decide you would like personalized guidance to help you with your womb healing, I invite you to apply for a call to chat with me by following the link or scanning the code:

https://wombhealing.ohmymamabody.com/5stepstechnique-bookcall

I'm here to help you to improve your fertility naturally.

Much love,
Vicki

PART ONE

YOUR FORGOTTEN INNER POWER

CHAPTER ONE

REALITY CHECK

"When you fall in love with your womb, you fall in love with life."

- Vicki Renz

I never expected it, nobody does. Why should you? We only take notice of our womb when we feel pain or experience imbalance.

That moment when you have the scan and the doctor's face maybe changes to a more focused look of concern and he says, "there's something here that needs attention...". It comes as such a shock.

You have a look. You can see it on their ultrasound picture. You can just about make out a little mass that's blocking your womb but at this point you don't really know much more than that.

But all of a sudden, your mind starts spinning all sorts of stories. It goes into a mode of fear and anxiety. You find yourself thinking: “What is this inside of me?”. “Is it something bad?”. “Is something bad going to happen to me?”. “Is it going to grow and get worse?”. “Will I have to have it cut out and is that going to hurt?”. “What if I am infertile?”.

Some wonder if their period is ever going to come back whilst others fear a heavy, painful period. Many more struggle with unexplained infertility; trying to get pregnant yet nothing seems to be working.

And the whole time it’s there in the back of your mind. Every single day you hold on to your womb trying to figure things out, asking yourself if it has got bigger or if your struggles have gotten worse. You find that you just can't concentrate on your everyday life.

And gradually over time it starts to really affect your quality of life; constantly feeling broken on the inside and distanced from your friends and close ones.

Many ladies say they feel lacking on the inside as their body is not working as it should. Physical symptoms such as bloating or what looks like bloating is embarrassing for them. For some, their lower abdomen starts to grow outwards, almost looking pregnant. And then of course having to face the comments of people wondering if you are pregnant. “Why didn't you tell us?”.

How do you respond to that? Because you're not pregnant. Instead, you are struggling with blockages in your womb and you're not feeling good at all in the slightest.

You start covering yourself up with the kind of clothes you're wearing. Something that's baggy. You don't want to go out socializing much anymore because you don't feel comfortable.

Your struggles really take away your self-esteem and how you feel about yourself. Your confidence is at an all time low, which isn't how the normal you would be at all.

You start looking online for possible causes for your blockages and your searches take you down a rabbit warren of dark scenarios. This only gives rise to feeling more nervous and anxious. So, you look online again with a different search term, hoping that your symptoms aren't that bad and instead discover more frightening outcomes.

Perhaps you've looked online and tried all sorts of suggested techniques already to unblock your womb:

- ▲ Fitness, if it's not causing you pain.
- ▲ Changing your diet, although that doesn't seem to do much.
- ▲ Yoga or acupuncture which helps to relax you, but only for the short term.

These all help you to feel healthy and more positive, yet they don't improve things on the inside.

You've noticed that your symptoms seem aggravated when you are feeling stressed - which has been quite a lot recently. Even though you try to relieve your stress with gentle activities, it feels like a vicious circle because your mind kicks in with overthinking which in turn leads to anxious feelings and thoughts.

Over time as your blockages persist, perhaps you get the feeling like something else is invading your body. You feel like this isn't a part of you, this doesn't belong to you because you are normally so outgoing, strong and driven.

These feelings start to open up your world to the holistic side of things. You find yourself thinking "is there another way?". "Another way that I can heal my womb?". "Is it possible to heal my fertility blockages naturally without possible surgery and further pain?".

"Can I get my cysts to shrink and disappear naturally?".

You don't want to continue your life in this way as it is really getting you down. You feel like you don't have control over your body. It's a harsh reality check for you that sometimes things happen in life that you don't have control over.

In my case I couldn't think of a life without getting pregnant and having children. It was something that I had always had in my life plan for myself.

Until my 30's I wasn't feeling ready for children. I'd even been in a previous marriage and society kind of expects that a married couple will have kids by the time they are 30.

I stopped being able to imagine having my children with him. Even though we were in love at the beginning, something changed in my life and I couldn't imagine having children with this guy anymore.

As I grew spiritually with my energy healing journey, we grew apart. I'd found self-love from within rather than looking for it outside of myself. Half of me was kind of scared as I was getting towards 30. It was a massive decision to leave this relationship but there was no way I could stay because there was no way I could have had children with him.

So, I made that bold move. I had to deeply trust in my journey and trust in following my path, even if I didn't know where it was taking me. Shortly after, I was enjoying a weekend away and that is when I met my now husband. We were both full of energy, adventure and traveling. We were far from ready for children as we were planning a trip around the world as backpackers.

A big shock came when I got pregnant by accident. At that time, I was wearing an IUD coil. Somehow the coil had fallen out. I hadn't realized until what I thought was my period just continued with light bleeding. It continued well past my standard five days of bleeding.

My partner said I should go to see the gynecologist, which is a pretty standard thing to do in Germany. You don't go to a General Practitioner doctor first; you go straight to "the lady doctor".

The gynecologist performed an internal ultrasound - something I had never had done in my life up until now and that in itself was a very intrusive experience. The ultrasound showed that I had a baby growing which was measuring around six weeks pregnant. I couldn't believe it. I knew something had felt different but I thought I was wearing a coil. So how could I be pregnant?

I wasn't ready for it either. We weren't ready! We were about to go traveling. I didn't really think much of it at the time because I was ready for adventure. I miscarried at around 8 weeks. Even though it was a huge upheaval and very traumatic, it just felt like it wasn't my time. I wanted to go traveling and see the world.

I still had to go through it all; lying in hospital having a dilation and curettage (D&C) operation (which I was totally unprepared for and have since created YouTube videos to help other women with this), feeling empty and lonely and lost.

I didn't feel like I could talk to anybody about it. It was 2010, there was no Instagram with groups of people going through miscarriage. Facebook was really young. The support groups weren't out there like they are now.

I simply lay there in the hospital...in the maternity ward, listening to newborn babies crying. It wasn't a good time in my life. But I was ready to live my life to go on that adventure to grasp everything that I could and make the most out of it.

It was a big wake up call and reality check. Reality hits in after losing a baby and you realize that time ticks away. A couple of years later when I was feeling ready in myself for my babies, I wasn't at all expecting fertility struggles.

There were days, very dark days when I didn't want to face the world. I could get pregnant but not stay pregnant. Experiencing tell-tale cramping and then bleeding, sometimes gushing, hiding away in the toilet and hoping that it wasn't happening again. Yet having to get up in the morning and keep on going and doing my job. I had to keep the income coming in which meant putting on a brave face and showing up.

I felt like I was living like a shadow of myself and no one else understood me. I was so emotional and all over the place. It was awful. I just wanted to hide and lock myself away from the whole world, which wasn't the normal me at all.

I felt jealous of all the women that had it so easy. Babies seemed to come so easily to others. I couldn't understand why the world was so unfair. Asking myself, "what have I done wrong?" and often wondering if I was cursed for leaving my previous marriage. All sorts of crazy thoughts went through my head.

I knew I didn't want to carry on that way. After three miscarriages I was eligible to get fertility tests done which involved driving to a top fertility clinic in Heidelberg every week to get blood tests and other internal checks carried out after the D&C operation.

I remember the ultrasound so clearly that it showed I had an ovarian cyst. It hadn't been there before because with each miscarriage I had had ultrasounds in order to check that my womb was clear.

It was another shock, seeing a mass of something inside of my womb. The doctors didn't say much other than they would keep an eye on it...but my mind was saying a lot! My thoughts started spinning all sorts of negative scenarios. What was going to happen now?

All of my other tests and checks had been fine and the doctors had given me the label of "unexplained infertility". They couldn't help me further and now this cyst had appeared out of nowhere.

At this point, something in the back of my mind flickered back into life. I remembered when I started a healing certification in my early twenties, I'd had this strange mass under the skin of my shin bone. My teacher at the time had taught me that the body gives physical signs when something is out of balance in our energy field and needs healing.

I remember my friends thinking I was crazy when I told them this and that I was working on healing this mass because it was holding negative emotions. Yet I continued because I trusted and believed in the path my life was taking me on. Sure enough it disappeared after I'd concentrated on healing the area myself.

This was the positive turning point in my fertility journey. That memory flickering back to life was showing me, reminding me that there were other ways to heal. I started working on my vision for my life ahead. I got back into my energy healing work.

I traveled deep within my body to discover the energies, the trauma that was still being held on to inside my womb. I started doing that self work that I had learned through my healing courses and practices in my twenties.

Discovering what I was holding onto deep within the cellular memory of my womb, understanding why I was holding on to these energies so that I could work on healing and releasing them. There was a huge amount to shift, which I thought I had already healed during my early twenties, but as I (and you will to) discovered with healing is that there are many layers of pain and trauma to shift through.

There is a point in your life where things click and you realize you can't stay in that place of sadness, despair and negativity any more. It’s what can be described as an inner voice, your inner guidance telling you that life is here to be lived.

Are you feeling your inner guidance? It’s probably what brought you to reading these pages. You would like to understand how to heal your womb. You feel like there must be another way than everything you have tried so far because others are doing it too.

So, what is womb healing? What's it all about? How's it going to help you to clear your blockages and to get your fertility flowing again?

You're here because you are ready to take those steps into the world of energy healing. You are open to understanding the energies behind your blockages so that you can support your body to naturally release those heavy energies, start flowing and get your quality of life back again.

I'm not the only one who has achieved such results from womb healing.

Here are 4 examples from some of my incredible clients of how my 5 Steps to Womb Healing technique can help you to heal and release your blockages in your womb:

Case Study One - Iris sets boundaries and ignites her powerful feminine spark
Iris first came to me like many of my clients do: - Feeling anxious about her cysts and the threat of surgery - Self criticism at an all time high, crushing her spirit - No longer wanting to socialize - Repetitive negative patterns in relationships Like many of my clients, Iris was a busy and successful career woman. She had worked hard to get where she was at and was great at what she did. Her frustration was that her personal life and how she felt on the inside didn't reflect her business life. She was feeling disillusioned with life and even though she had put a lot of effort into a healthy lifestyle, she still had her cyst which was causing her to feel inadequate as a woman. So we got to work getting Iris unstuck from the heavy energies within her cyst by implementing my 5 Steps to Womb Healing technique. Within sixty days, she had become a lot lighter and positivity was flowing as she had released a huge amount of blockages associated

with her childhood and ex partners.

Then things really started to shift positively in her life. Once that sluggish, stagnant energy had been massively released, she was open to embracing her spirit, passions and true drive in life.

You see, once we had cleared that heavy energy which was causing her to be blocked, feel inadequate and disillusioned, we had opened up her energy field, igniting her inner feminine flow so that she found her spark.

It was like a butterfly emerging from a cocoon. She stepped into a place of empowerment; setting clear boundaries energetically and verbally, speaking up and creating change in her life. Was she nervous, yes! But she had self belief and inner strength to fuel her, which had been missing before.

Her work colleagues were getting used to this new person, saying how good she looks and genuinely taking interest in her as a person rather than just pushing work in her direction. She gained new respect and authority.

It goes to show just how much of what is going on inside can affect us on the outside.

Iris's story doesn't end there, she is only just getting started and you can imagine how motivated she is to continue in her new found positive flow as her life truly blossoms all around her.

If this is the kind of thing you bought this book hoping

to discover, you'll be feeling really eager to jump into the practical exercises for your womb healing in The Five Steps to Womb Healing chapters.

It takes consistency to work on yourself to heal and release your blockages in your womb, but once you ignite your positive flow, the difference it will make in your life is remarkable.

Case Study Two – Chloe goes from endless TTC to pregnancy after her leap of faith

Chloe's story is an inspiring one for those looking to finally get pregnant after what feels like endless months of trying to conceive.

Chloe found my website whilst searching online for techniques to get pregnant naturally. She followed one of my guided meditations and started using my free 5 Steps Guide straightaway.

After already experiencing some breakthroughs from connecting with and sending her womb love, she reached out to me on Instagram. I invited her to one of my first womb healing workshops as she really wanted to try it out with me live.

She just knew there was more to her fertility struggles on an energetic level. She clearly felt that she must be holding on to energies which were blocking her not only in her womb but in many areas of life.

At first Chloe was unsure about how womb healing could really make a difference. She even says herself that she soon learnt just how much of a positive difference it makes!

She absolutely loved my Womb Vitality workshop and a couple of weeks later we had a 1:1 call. She was still feeling unsure about joining my Tribe. There was some fear of the unknown holding her back...we all know what that feels like!

Chloe followed my guidance on Instagram and YouTube closely. It gave her more confidence and inspiration to keep on working on herself and unblocking the energies that were in her womb.

A few weeks later she took a leap of faith and joined my Tribe. Chloe came to all of the sessions and listened to the recordings many times, consistently doing her self love work and feeling herself in an accelerated growth spurt on many levels in life.

It felt like that leap of faith was the key to unlocking her flow. Just a few weeks later, Chloe got her positive pregnancy test! So beautiful.

She continued in my Tribe throughout her pregnancy, which helped her enormously to shift through anxieties, grow in confidence, find her voice and set clear boundaries.

Like Iris, Chloe really found her spark and stepped into her confident feminine power. So much so that she shares her story via video on my YouTube channel, sharing her story to inspire you.

Watch here or scan the code below:

Case Study Three - Charlotte gets back her regular cycle, kicking PCOS in the butt

Charlotte found me on YouTube as she kept on experiencing pregnancy symptoms but only getting negative tests. She had been trying to conceive again about a year after her first son was born, but things weren't working out. She frequently felt pregnant and her period would be late...but still no pregnancy.

She was feeling in a negative headspace; it seemed like everyone around her was getting pregnant but she wasn't, which was making her feel jealous, bitter and hopeless with all of her tracking, symptom checking and testing month in and month out.

She decided to go for a check up at the doctor and was diagnosed with PCOS. Polycystic Ovarian Syndrome is a hormonal imbalance which can cause women not to ovulate and create small cysts on the ovaries. Other symptoms are irregular or missed periods, facial hair, infertility and weight gain.

Women coming to me with PCOS just feel terrible; unworthy as a woman, even embarrassed and ashamed because of their body. They just want to get rid of their imbalance and get their quality of life back again.

Charlotte completely embraced her womb healing journey. Our first session took her into a deep remembering of her birth trauma from her first son. It had been buried deep within and as a result was causing her energy flow to be blocked.

It takes a lot of courage to heal trauma and release it. My 5 Steps Technique helps you to do this from a place of love and protection. My clients feel held and supported as they go through their layers of healing, coming out of the other side feeling lighter and glowing.

Charlotte was very determined to heal and implemented her favorite womb healing techniques into a daily routine for herself. You can imagine her elation as her menstrual cycle and hormones regulated and she found her balance.

She personally said that she started to feel like the best version of herself and much clearer with daily journaling and positive manifestation.

This comes from connecting deeply with your womb energy, healing and releasing your blockages and allowing your true feminine to flow.

The technique you learn in this book will change the energies in your womb and impact your life positively.

Remember, it takes consistency as healing is like peeling the layers of an onion; the deeper you go, the more is revealed and the healing process is repeated.

Although my clients feel immediate lightness and a shift in energy after their first session, this is just the peak of the iceberg.

Case Study Four - Maria gets her period back and gets the all clear

Maria found me via my YouTube videos, as she was searching for information around fibroids and cysts. She saw I was holding a Womb Healing Mastery workshop and signed up. She experienced almost immediate shifts after connecting with her womb.

Maria booked an initial 1:1 call with me straight after attending my workshop. She had really enjoyed my 5 Step Technique and felt instinctively that my womb healing technique was the key to shifting her blocked flow and draining negative patterns in her life.

Maria had already worked with several therapists and tried out natural healing techniques throughout her adult life yet nothing really seemed to be bringing her the lasting vitality, life fulfillment, sexual and relationship life she was after. After attending my workshop she instinctively knew that womb healing would help her as it focuses directly on the area where the problem is.

When she first spoke with me she was mainly concerned about relationship issues, isolation and fears of infertility. She was feeling so frustrated and blocked because her period hadn't shown up for over two months. Negative patterns kept showing up in her life and she just wanted to finally shake free of them. Plus, to add to her stress, she had recently been for a cervical smear and the results had come back indicating that GC cells (Atypical Glandular Cells) had been detected, that can be indications of cancer or other serious conditions.

During our call I took her through a deeper womb connection exercise which guided her to start releasing energetic ties which were keeping her attached to negative experiences in her life. Straightaway she felt lighter.

Maria became a 1:1 client and also joined my Tribe immediately after our call.

One week later Maria got her period back. What an elation for her! I am sure you can empathize if you have experienced the frustration of missed periods and not getting that release and reset each month.

Due to her AGC results, Maria had been requested to go in for a small biopsy (colposcopy). We worked intensively on the energy within the cells in the area and Maria herself felt that it was cleared. She continued with the biopsy in order to get clear medical data. It was painful and it took some days to recover whilst sending loving energy to her womb. Thankfully her results came back normal.

Since working with me 1:1, Maria has had her period every single month. She attends as many of my Tribe sessions as she can live and is highly motivated to continue working on releasing the layers of energetic blockages in her womb. Her results so far are just the beginning of her womb healing journey. She does feel also more energetic, happy, peaceful and social that gives her hope to reach her desires in intimate relationships as well in the near future.

That's what happens when you start discovering the energies in your womb and experiencing transformational releases; you just feel so joyful and clear that you can create positive change in your life.

"I am so happy I cannot believe it. Like a 1000 year old weight has been lifted off my shoulders.

I feel alive, which is really what I was looking for so long to get out of this halfway dead life feeling."

You know...many ladies struggling with missed periods have gotten their period back following on from just one womb healing session with me.

My Five Steps Technique guides you to heal at cellular level, releasing deep stress and reviving the communication between your brain and your reproductive system, bringing hormonal balance and flow.

Medical Disclaimer

Womb Healing is a complementary energy healing technique based on the energy field in the body. It is in no way a replacement for any kind of medical advice and support.

You are advised to continue to take medical advice and consult your doctor throughout your womb healing journey.

As you have read from my personal story, I was undergoing regular medical checks throughout my fertility journey. We need the medical side for clear, factual data as well as the ultrasounds.

Womb healing works on an energetic level, connecting with cellular memory within your womb so that you can heal trauma and bring in positive flow.

Combining womb healing and medical advice gives you the whole picture of your overall well-being. In this way you are supporting yourself energetically whilst also receiving that important medical support and advice.

Results described in the Case Studies are from clients who worked 1:1 with me and who took consistent daily action to further their healing progress between our sessions.

CHAPTER TWO

WAKING UP TO YOUR WOMB

"When your thoughts and feelings vibrate at a high level, so too do the cells in your body."

- Vicki Renz

During the earlier days of my fertility struggles I had pushed my energy work, my healing techniques to one side. Trauma, depression, sadness and the loneliness of my fertility journey had taken over my life.

In my early 20's I had joined the dots, what felt like a massive discovery at the time, connecting them to me being an intuitive healer. As a child I'd often known things before they'd happened. I could sense all those energies around me.

I'd never really known how to cope with it properly or what was really going on. I had often thought that people just didn't like me when in actual fact I was picking up on their inner struggles! Kind of like a radar.

It was whilst working in London that I met a lovely friend who introduced me to energy healing. I started to study my first ever healing course with the National Federation of Spiritual Healers (NFSH) in the UK. I learnt how to guide and channel energies to help others with their energy fields. I met others like me.

My healing studies really opened me up to the world of understanding that our bodies are made up of energies. What's more, this is all scientifically proven. Not so "woo woo" after all!

Scientists have proven that the organs in our body hold on to memory. It is termed as "cellular memory".

So as you can imagine, if we have a lot of negative traumatic cellular memory, then our body is going to be weak. It's not going to function at 100%.

By connecting with our internal energy flow and guiding our body to release those heavier energies related to trauma, old pain, old negative patterns, emotions that are stored within ourselves and the organs in our bodies, we're helping our body to charge up with positivity.

We need positive flow for everything inside for our body to work as it should do. Think about a violin that is out of tune or cannot be played properly. It makes an awful sound and you cover your ears to protect yourself from the discord. When the same violin is tuned up and played well, it creates a beautiful sound as it sends out a vibration of harmony. It's exactly the same with us; constantly being busy and stressed creates inner discord.

When we take the time to be still and tune in with ourselves, we immediately feel good as we are in harmony with our inner flow. By going within, you discover where you are out of tune (your blockages) and take action to re-tune to the vibration that creates your inner positivity.

For a while I worked at a drop-in center in southwest London. Many people came in once a week for energy healing. As a qualified NFSH healer I guided the energy through their bodies to help them to “charge up their engines”, to optimize their flow.

Seeing how many people were coming in, open for energy healing started to change my life. I moved away from the area. There was so very much for me to learn. During my travels, I started learning with a beautiful healer called “CC” in America. She was a shamanic healer, very connected to nature which brought in a lot of earthiness to my healing techniques. I studied with her for many years, learning techniques from Barbara Brennan where CC had been a student.

During my travels, one of my favorite places was Peru. Being up at 4000 meters and even higher, feeling free and connected with nature. Whilst in Cuzco I went for a lovely energy healing using sound. It was the first time that I'd had a sound energy healing and really felt the vibrations in my body responding and healing with the sound I was receiving.

Our bodies are heavily influenced by energy waves and sound vibrations. The female human body is made up of 55% water. Scientific experiments provide visual evidence of how water responds to sound.

Experiments show how water molecules create patterns and change shape when certain tones of music are played. It's absolutely amazing. We can see these patterns when we study snowflakes. A negative tone shows a pattern that we perceive as looking ill or out of balance.

When we dig deeper into this, we can understand how much energy and vibration affects how we optimally flow as a human being.

Why is all of this energy stored in our womb space?

I love to call our womb our second heart. Think about how easy it is to connect in with our heart. We clearly feel the emotions of love, heaviness, sadness within our heart. We feel connected with our hearts pretty much every day; when you see something that fills you with compassion, you feel it in your heart. When you hear something upsetting, you feel it in your heart.

Our wombs carry this energy as well. Can you feel it in your womb?

Most women associate pain, soreness and heaviness with their womb. In many societies, menstruation is shrouded with pain and shame, often being referred to as the "women's curse".

It wasn't always this way. Our wombs are a creative vessel that bring life forth to our Earth. When we look at tribal cultures who are deeply connected with ancient customs, we see that women are celebrated. Menstruation is viewed as something sacred and powerful.

Did you know that a healthy, flowing menstruation is not normally painful? Any pain associated with our womb is our womb crying out for us to listen to her. Yet we ignore our womb, perhaps take some painkillers and carry on with our busy lives.

As we continue with our busy lives we become more and more distanced and disconnected from our second heart, from our inner wisdom, from our core feminine flow. It's time for you to connect and change this around.

It's time for you to listen to your womb. She has been sending you signs. She's been trying to communicate with you. And now you're here to discover how to listen and understand what's being held onto deep within.

A very common negative pull on our womb energy is from previous partners. We don't realize we hold on to those energies. There is a lot more to a previous relationship than just walking away. We share our womb space with our partners which creates an energy bond.

We can't see this bond with our eyes but we can feel it on an energetic level. This bond drains us and we continue, unknowingly, to give a lot of our energy away. When we understand just how much we are giving away and learn how we can release these bonds, we reclaim so much of our inner power.

We store so much cellular memory in our womb because it is our feminine core. These could be experiences affecting our femininity, our confidence in self, how we felt as a child, our time in the womb where we absorbed our mother's cellular memory and much more.

So many ladies who work with me say they feel the immediate lightness. They start to remember who they truly are, their feminine flow. Releasing energetic bonds opens the door to their true self, they start doing things they love doing, things that they're so passionate about.

It could be singing, dancing, creating something, going out for amazing walks in nature. Something they've just kind of been putting to one side and all of a sudden, this amazing urge comes back and they're off reclaiming their lives!

An awakening to their feminine core takes place, a transformation; glowing again, shining, getting back their true self simply because they're releasing so many ties from their wombs. Claiming back their energy. Not letting others influence them or drain them anymore.

That's just a small part of awakening your womb and claiming back your energy. It goes so much deeper than this...which is why I absolutely love guiding you to connect with and unblock your womb with the Five Steps Technique.

CHAPTER THREE

WHO THIS BOOK IS FOR?

"I love to call our wombs our second heart, she feels emotions in the same way we feel emotions in our heart."

- Vicki Renz

You're struggling with physical blockages or imbalance in your womb such as ovarian cysts, irregular periods, fibroids, heavy periods, endometriosis...just to name a few of the struggles women are having to cope with on a daily basis.

On top of that you are constantly fighting with your inner critic which may well be causing you anxiety.

You really would like to heal naturally and you've heard about womb healing and energy healing. You're not really sure exactly how it's going to work but you're very open to trying it on yourself because it just feels like everything else you’ve tried so far isn't working.

You want to get back your quality of life because your struggles are affecting you so much.

This book is for you if you're ready to work on yourself consistently by putting my womb healing techniques into your daily routine, being consistent with your healing routine and patient with yourself.

Womb healing is something that works on the energetic level in your body, which means it takes time to gradually change things and get positive results.

You are going to be learning something new. You will be reprogramming your cellular memory and getting into a new routine. You will be programming your mind to get into a new way of doing things. Research shows that it normally takes us two months to consistently implement a new habit into our lives so that it becomes automatic to us. Are you feeling ready to work on yourself daily?

With my womb healing techniques you will not only be creating a new routine, you will be reprogramming your energy flow positively.

Once you start connecting with and really understanding your womb, it's like opening up a whole new conversation. Think about it being like getting to know someone:

- First of all we notice what they look like, their main features and get a general first impression.

- When you meet again you may ask a couple of questions and get to know them a little better but still at surface level.
- During the next few times you meet, you open up a bit more and learn more about each other, you connect, you have deeper conversations.

This works exactly the same way with your womb connection. The more you get to trust, the more confident you get. The more consistent you are with opening up that channel of communication, really understanding what you're holding on to within, the more you can heal and release.

Your womb healing journey takes determination and it takes motivation. It's not a case of "oh, I'll read the Guide through now and think about it later". It's not going to change things for you just by reading through. You can only change things by taking consistent action. Trusting yourself and believing that the actions you are taking are transforming the energy flow in your life.

You know there is a lot behind tapping into your energies to heal your womb.

You're open to understanding and implementing my womb healing techniques so that you can get back your quality of life.

Now, many women do choose to join me in my WOMMB Tribe (that stands for Women's Oh My Mama Body) for continued ongoing motivation because they find it hard to go on their own. They love to have that input of personal guidance from me with regular techniques to really be in the healing energy space to keep their womb healing momentum going.

We come together as a group every single week, sharing the space with other women who understand each other, women who are going through similar struggles and healing.

It's so important to make that time for yourself every single day.

Do you have a strong urge from within to get back your quality of life? To feel amazing about yourself, to feel confidence and strength? The Five Step Technique gives you the determination to keep you going. It's why you're here in the first place.

This is for you, if you're really ready to turn around those blockages in your womb space by learning how my womb techniques work and how you can consistently apply them on yourself so that you heal and release.

Womb Connection Check In Exercise

Before we proceed with the rest of the book, let's first check in with where you're at right now with your womb connection and self worth.

Below, rate yourself on a scale from 1 - 5 on how accurate the statements are

- 1 means "not accurate at all," and
- 5 means "most accurate"

Once you've rated yourself for each statement, total up your scores and then use the Answer Key to determine your next steps.

Check in Statement	Self Rating
When I look at myself in the mirror I like what I see	
When I wake up in the morning I feel motivated to start my day	
I have a morning routine which sets me up positively for my day ahead	
Upon waking I connect with my inner self before I turn on any electronic devices	
My inner voice is positive and encourages me	
I know how to connect with my womb	
I connect with my womb daily and send love to her	
I know when I am out of balance and have techniques which I can implement to get my balance back	
I feel happy about my childhood and have great memories	
I feel at peace with past relationships	

I have a great relationship with my parents	
I know what my passions are and spend time on them daily	
I have time for self care and it is important to me to have this time for myself daily	
If I feel stressed I know what works best for releasing stress from my body, mind and soul	

Score 0 - 30
Stuck Energies are Holding You Back

The bad news is that your womb energy is stagnant and is harboring a build up of negative energy. Not only is this causing heaviness and blockages on the inside, it is showing up on the outside and you are feeling disconnected from life.

You probably already know and feel this every day. No surprise there.

However, the good news is that you can turn all of this around positively, and even better, you get to re-energize your routines and relationships, bringing in lightness from the moment you wake up in the morning.

Read this book with an open mind. Consider how implementing the Five Steps to Womb Healing Technique could radically improve your energy flow. It won't take much for you to experience a revived positive flow.

Score 31 - 45
A Positive, Consistent Routine Will Lighten Your Life

If your score landed here, it means your daily routine is what is holding you back from enjoying a consistent positive flow in your life.

You likely have a routine but often fall out of it. Let me guess...you have really good intentions and yet the busyness of everyday life takes over and before you know it, another week has gone by. You never intend to scroll through your phone immediately upon waking but once again you have slipped into it.

Finding a good motivation for you to get into a routine that you well and truly stick to will allow you, for the first time, to experience deep healing. You'll start connecting with your true self and rediscovering your passions. You'll be so motivated to plan time in your busy calendar for self-love (womb healing), you'll soon be flowing with positive energy and easily on your way to getting back your quality of life.

Score 46 - 59
You're on a Good Track and Can Easily Unleash Your Positive Flow

You've got your main morning routine in place and are super consistent with self care. You know which techniques to use if you're having "one of those days" and you can really feel the difference in your life.

For you, the biggest hurdle to overcome is digging deep enough into your womb to release negative energies. You can feel the positive shifts in your life since you started implementing self care techniques, yet you often feel like you are not getting to the bottom of things. Some aspects of your life are still really bothering you. You still feel like something is stuck but can't quite put your finger on it.

This is where the Five Steps to Womb Healing Technique comes in. You'll learn how to deeply connect and communicate with your womb energy. As you peel away at the layers, you'll discover the root causes behind your blockages that have been holding you back from flowing. You'll gradually dig deeper and feel your positive flow being more and more unleashed with each and every womb healing.

Score 60+
You Just Need to Heal and Release a Deeply Lingering Energy

You've healed and released so many layers of heavy energy, you really have done a lot of self work. Yet you are frustrated because your womb continues to be blocked, despite your best efforts.

You really feel like you have done enough healing, having tried several therapies and gained some good results. You understand that our body holds energies which is why you are so consistent with your daily self care.

Yet deep down, something hasn't healed and you're determined to get to the bottom of things and finally release that lingering, heavy energy.

My Five Step Womb Healing Technique guides you to focus on the energies stored in your womb. Many healing techniques work wonders yet they completely miss out our feminine core! Our womb space. Our second heart.

Once you deeply connect in with your womb and listen to her, allowing her to communicate to you what is behind your blockages, then you will receive a profound understanding of what is being held at a cellular level. No doubt you'll experience a swift transformation once you discover what those deep, lingering energies are because you are already in your healing flow.

You'll finally be able to heal at a deep, cellular level. Your womb will be vibrating with a revived positive energy within each and every cell, fully reviving your positive flow.

CHAPTER FOUR

STRUGGLES WE ALL FACE

"We often feel triggered and challenged. When we choose to view these situations as opportunities for healing and growth, this is where the magic happens."

- Vicki Renz

1. Disconnectedness with Self

Modern society has us almost constantly plugged into external inputs and on the go. Our brain is so active and working on processing inputs that we are living more in our mind than in our body.

On top of this we are surrounded by electro-smog from radio waves, electronic signals from Wifi, mobile phones, laptops...and much more. So even when we think we have a quiet moment, we are still receiving input.

On a typical day, upon waking in the morning, our phone is plugged in next to our bed. We turn on a light. As we gradually wake up and want to start getting ready for our day we see our phone and the first thing we want to do is check it for messages and updates in social media.

We turn it on and we're already getting lost in a world of other people. The news creeps in and what's going on in the world starts to drain your energy.

Then we think about our day ahead. What have we got planned for the day ahead? Okay, it's a busy day at work and you can feel the pressure of your to-do list. Then there's a problem we are facing and it starts to create thoughts in our mind as we think about how to deal with it.

The momentum speeds up. We are being bombarded from all angles with all of these external events, stressors, negative energies, and it's pulling us down. Our active mind is completely blocking us from being within our body and connecting in with our energy flow.

Can you feel that disconnectedness within yourself? We have come to the point where we only notice our body if we have aches and pains.

How often during the day do you really take time for yourself where you connect in with your body? Is it a short walk? Meditation? Yoga?

Do you know how many hours you sit at your computer? Do you track how many hours you spend on your phone?

Think about how many hours you are completely occupied with other people and business rather than looking after yourself? As well as the accumulated electro smog which has a direct impact on your energy field.

Now think about this question: How much time do you truly, deeply spend on your own self, on your connectedness with your inner flow? What does your body feel like when you connect in? What about your womb?

Here are 5 Daily Tips for you to become more connected with your body:

1. Reduce electro-smog whilst you sleep by disconnecting all electronic devices and removing the plugs from the sockets in the wall. You may choose to use EMF protection stickers to improve your energy field.
2. Set yourself a clear time every evening to turn off your phone or leave it on airplane mode.
3. Keep your phone turned off in the morning until you have completed your morning routine (more tips on this later).
4. Upon waking, immediately connect in with your heart and your womb before allowing any thoughts of the day to creep in. These couple of minutes connecting in will make a huge positive impact on your day ahead. See Chapter "Continuing Forward"

for a guided exercise on this.

Whilst connecting in with your heart and your womb, focus on (at least) three feelings of gratitude - what are you grateful for in your life, at this moment - feeling the flow of that energy in your body

2. Inner Critic

We all have one of these! A little voice inside of our head that questions us, judges us, gives us a hard time, challenges us with questions of "what if". Some days it's loud and other days we hardly notice it.

How do you speak with yourself on the inside? When you see yourself in the mirror do you greet yourself cheerfully or do you pick out things that you are not happy with about yourself? What about when you're getting dressed?

Do you truly feel good about yourself? Or is that inner critic voice in full swing, pulling you down, picking out every single little imperfection on your face? Perhaps your voice criticizes how you are dressed?

It may be that you have a blemish or a spot on your face that's not going to look good today. Your inner critic makes you aware of it the whole day long; feeling self-conscious about that tiny little thing on your face that probably no one else even notices or if they do it lasts as a thought for 1 millisecond because they too have their own inputs running at a hundred miles an hour in their own head.

Is your inner voice holding you back? You would love to say something but you feel like you can't. It's just not coming out, it's blocked and you feel under stress or shaky at the thought of speaking out loud. Or if you do say something your inner voice starts to over analyze the whole conversation afterwards, “oh my gosh, why did I say that?” Or “what did he think about me”, or “what did she think when she looked at me?”.

Do you feel like you are under a constant barrage from your inner critic? Your own mind is pulling you down. Can you imagine if your inner critic was an actual person? They would be called a narcissist!

There is a great technique where you name your inner critic. For example, by giving your inner critic a name like “Critical Christine”. You can speak to her directly and tell her “not now Christine” or “be quiet Christine, I don't need your opinion right now”.

It works wonders!

You can quieten “Christine” and then call in your inner positive, strengthening yourself and reaffirming to yourself “yes, this is who I am”, “this is my flow”, “this is who I am meant to be”. You can already feel the change in energy as you are reading this.

I recommend you give your positive side a name too such as “Positive Pippa”. Pippa is lovely and says things like; “this is what you love doing”, “I really love you”, “you’re good at this”, ‘you’ve got this”. Pippa is your cheerleader, motivating you and encouraging you to believe in yourself.

Each lady who comes to me says that they really struggle with the inner battle with their thoughts. They find it hard to work on their womb healing by themselves and much prefer the encouragement, motivation and positivity of working with me 1:1 or in my Tribe.

They especially love my weekly guided embodied journaling technique where I help them to strengthen their inner positive and self belief. Having regular supportive techniques available to them in my Tribe helps to stop their inner critic from creeping back in again and again.

Short Exercise For Naming Your Inner Critic and Your Inner Positive

1. Start by giving your inner critic a name: "Critical *NAME*"
    a. Give a name that suits your inner critic well
2. Think about your inner critic, what does she typically tell you? List at least five common things she says to you...here are some examples:
    a. "This is happening because you're not good enough"
    b. "You may as well give up and stop wasting your time"
    c. "Who cares about you anyway"
    d. "What if things come up during healing that will make you feel worse? Best to play it safe and not get into it"

   e. "You're inadequate as a woman"
3. Prepare yourself with five responses for your inner critic so that you can quickly stop her in her tracks...here are some examples:
   a. "Be quiet "Critical *NAME*", stop being so unkind"
   b. "You know that's not true "Critical *NAME*""
   c. "Not right now "Critical *NAME*""
   d. "Give me some space "Critical *NAME*""
   e. "That's enough "Critical *NAME*""
4. Give your positive inner voice a name "Positive *NAME*"
5. Your "Positive *NAME*" is your cheerleader! Think about five positive, motivational statements that she can support you with...here are some examples:
   a. "You are more than worthy"
   b. "Keep on going, you've already come so far and are doing so well"
   c. "I'm so proud of you"
   d. "You've faced challenges before and grown from them, I know you can get through this one too"
   e. "You are an incredible, amazing woman"
6. I recommend calling in "Positive *NAME*" after you've sent "Critical *NAME*" away, using one (or more!) of her cheerleader statements to get you back into your positive flow. It's great to have these statements practiced and at the ready so you can quickly turn around any negative chatter.

3. Lack of Time

Time, or lack of it, is a massive problem for many. We are all so busy, every single moment of the day. There's always something to think about and something to do. Then our phone rings or vibrates with a message or update. It just doesn't stop. We are here, there and everywhere. Always things to do and places to go.

This busy life isn't actually intended for us. Our human design as it is today, is not built for the mass of information streaming at us. We hardly have time for our own thoughts. Life has changed so much for us as human beings compared to 100, 500, 1000 years ago. Look at how human beings lived then compared to how we live now. It is truly remarkable how busy we are.

Do you have the feeling that you never have enough time to do everything? You have so many good intentions to sit down and take ten minutes for yourself but then you get to the end of the day and realize that you got distracted or forgot and now you are too tired.

The great thing I would like to share with you is that time is something we can take back control of. We can choose to live at a fast pace or a slower pace. Even if we do have 1001 things to do every single day, we can choose how to prioritize our day and to fit that time in for ourselves.

I am assuming here that up until now you haven't done any womb energy healing techniques on yourself simply because you haven't had the time to sit down and understand how to do it. Or perhaps you have thought about 1:1 sessions but you don't have time in your calendar for that either. You simply don't have time.

I understand what it's like. In the current every day of our lives, something like womb healing doesn't take the place of priority number one. It's a "nice to have" because it's energy healing, something you can't put your finger on or see. Yet, what's happening in the longer term is that the ongoing build-up of stress is creating more strain on your reproductive system.

One of the most important things for us women is that our reproductive system functions at 100%. When we have stress in our lives, the stress hormone Cortisol is produced by our body. Cortisol gradually starts blocking messages between your brain and your womb. The job of Cortisol is to reduce the function of our reproductive system as a stressed womb is not a healthy environment for a baby to grow in.

Our reproductive system is vital for hormonal and holistic balance. Women have a cyclical nature due to the four phases of our menstrual cycle; menstruation, follicular phase, ovulation and luteal phase. Each phase is regulated by our hormones.

When our hormones are out of synchronization, we feel off balance, out of place. Our cycles may become irregular or we experience massive mood swings. We get even more stressed because we feel all over the place yet we don't really know why.

This is why time for connection with your womb is incredibly important for your overall balance and wellbeing. Unfortunately, it mostly takes something more serious to happen for us to pay attention to our womb.

Your womb feels painful, physical signs of imbalance such as ovarian cysts, endometriosis, fibroids show up or you have unexpected fertility struggles. All of a sudden you are aware of your womb and start to realize that maybe there is something more to this. Especially as you begin your journey to seeking natural healing techniques.

Investing time into womb connection is so important for you in the short term and the longer term. Ask yourself how much time you can make available? How much time do you feel you would need per day and each week?

Do you feel like you're struggling to find the time or is it a question of struggling to make the time?

Imagine the difference that just twenty minutes daily or perhaps one hour a week could make to your womb balance. With so many women getting back their menstruation after just one of my 1:1 sessions, simply by creating that communication with their womb, it really is worth investing your time so that you too can feel and experience the shifts that womb healing brings.

The more in tune you are with your womb, the more you can feel confident identifying if something is feeling out of balance and then take action by using my 5 Steps to Womb Healing Technique to heal, release and regain balance.

Once you deeply connect in with your womb, listening to her, allowing her to communicate to you what is behind your blockages, you will receive a profound understanding of the heavy energies being held at a cellular level. Regular womb connection will bring you into your healing flow and you will start to notice how much lighter you are starting to feel.

Over the weeks, the time you invest into your womb connection compounds. You'll start to notice that your womb is vibrating with a revived positive energy and that you yourself are feeling much more balanced and flowing.

Tips for Creating Time for Connecting With Your Womb

- ▲ Schedule appointments with yourself in your calendar and set the notification to alert you (I schedule 30 minute daily appointments for myself)
- ▲ Notice common distractions such as time lost scrolling through messages, looking at social media – become more aware of this and put your phone out of sight
- ▲ Implement womb connection into your daily routine, starting from the moment you wake up. See Chapter "Continuing Forward" for a guided exercise on this.
- ▲ Get motivation and support by joining my Tribe which has regular live events, recordings to suit your schedule as well as a circle of women all on a similar journey

Join one of my embodied journaling sessions to learn how to create positive mantras for yourself which are directly connected to your womb energy flow - you can use these mantras whilst making a cup of tea, doing odd jobs around the house - this all counts as you are creating positive energy in your womb

CHAPTER FIVE

WHY WOMB HEALING WORKS

"To find light, we also need to know what darkness is."

- Vicki Renz

Understanding Cellular Memory

When you learn how to connect and communicate with your womb you understand that your womb is holding on to trauma, pain and stress. Your womb will share emotions, feelings, memories and more with you as you get confident with communicating with her.

You've buried so much for such a long time which is why your womb is crying out to you with physical symptoms. Women have undergone surgery for their cysts only for them to grow back again. Why do they grow back? Simply cutting out a cyst takes away the physical problem for a while yet it does not heal the negative cellular level memory in your womb.

Many women coming to me have often come to this realization on their own. Womb healing guides you to connect with heavy energies which are the root cause behind your struggles.

You can do things like nourish and cleanse your body. You can be perfectly healthy on the outside. Yet all of this self care is not getting to your inner energy flow. This is why womb healing works because you are working to create a positive energy flow. You are cleansing your cellular memory.

Your cellular memory could be holding on to childhood trauma, relationship trauma, mother daughter relationship issues. Do you notice repetitive patterns showing up in your life? These are stuck energies. Perhaps you have inherited generational trauma passed down from generation to generation, negative beliefs that are deeply programmed within.

You can break the chains through your healing. You decide that the cells in your womb are no longer going to be carrying around these patterns. You can go in and release the energetic blueprints in your cells by understanding what it is that you are holding onto and working on healing them at an energetic level.

Imagine what it feels like to step into a positive, flowing, self-confident, strengthened, glowing energy. That childhood trauma no longer weighs you down, that relationship which you could never really move on from is soothed and released, you understand your parents better and can bring that younger you the love that she so needed when she was feeling sad and misunderstood.

You may be asking yourself why don't doctors work on this level? Why don't they understand cellular memory? Why do they recommend cutting things out or taking hormone regulators instead? Some western doctors are opening up to energy healing and recommend their clients to look into a more holistic approach to complement their medical recommendations.

Holistic Medicine

Chinese medicine is well known for channeling energy, "qi", through the body. Acupuncture works with the twelve energy meridians which are the basis for traditional Chinese medicine. A large number of the Chinese population practice the ancient exercise called "Qigong" which optimizes energy in the body, mind and spirit. Working with our energy flow is not something new, it is more that it is an ancient practice that has been forgotten in the modern western world.

Dr. Joe Dispenza is a well-known Chiropractor turned Neuroscientist who speaks internationally and teaches others the same technique he used to heal himself after breaking several vertebrae and being told he would never walk again. Dr. Joe Dispenza used the power of his mind and meditation to visualize his body healing.

Through his incredible healing experience, he was spurred on to study neuroscience where he discovered that our thoughts directly affect our body. Negative thoughts and experiences can directly impact our health. Negative experiences and trauma can gradually change our cells, leading to physical signs of imbalance. Women hold so much within their womb because it is their feminine energy center.

A further great international speaker and author, Dr. Wayne Dyer talked about our thoughts creating our reality. His most famous saying was “change your thoughts, change your life” and wrote many books on the subject.

People around the world are waking up to the power of energy healing. Something that, in western society, has been quietened down for such a long time. In fact, a huge amount of fear and negativity had been created around energy healing. Women were labeled as “witches” and energy healing as “black magic”, something dangerous and to fear. Thankfully the openness of the internet, excellent explanations and scientific studies are helping us to understand how energy really works within our body.

Shamanic Healing

One of my favorite healing techniques is shamanic healing. The word shaman is often associated with negativity, yet the shaman has been around for 1000s of years, the original tribal healer for people who were ill.

Shamanism is deeply connected to nature and understanding which plants provide healing medicines, as well as to the wisdom of the earth, the vibration of energy and healing with these energies. A typical tribal shaman goes into a trance to connect with these energies, something which for an outsider could seem scary, which is why it is shrouded in negativity, simply because the practice is very misunderstood.

Ask yourself how you feel when you hear the word “shaman”. We've been programmed to associate fear with it.

As shamanic healing is one of my favorite techniques, I would like to describe my take on it. Partly, shamanic healing is about connecting ourselves with the four elements of earth, air, fire and water. A further part of shamanic healing is using the rhythm of a drum to enter a trance-like state of awareness to perform a healing by seeing into the energy being held in someone and supporting them to release this.

My very first healing experience was with a shaman in London, perhaps that’s another reason why I love it so much. It opened up a whole new world to me as I started to understand that others could see energy flowing and energy blockages.

It wasn’t until my second son was born that I started to study shamanic healing and qualify myself. Whilst holding my son close to me I repeatedly saw visions which were related to where he had come from. They weren’t pleasant visions. At the time I asked a couple of my healer friends to support me in helping my son to release and heal from his past. Thankfully because of my healing work up until that point, I knew I wasn’t hallucinating!

Side note: if you know people with babies who are screaming a lot, it would be worth suggesting they look into energy healing for their baby.

When I work with ladies on a shamanic level, I guide them to visually travel to their womb so that they can discover the energies for themselves. I also travel into their womb and visualize the energy flow within. I receive what feels and looks like a channeled flow of healing energy which is guided to my client. This is why it also works brilliantly from distance, via video calling. I do not have to be sitting next to someone for this channeling of healing energy to work.

Women decide to work on a one to one basis with me because they are very interested in getting straight to the root cause of their problems or because they don't feel they are able to dig deep enough into the energies behind their blockages. They feel they don't have time to practice my Five Steps to Womb Healing Technique on themselves to heal effectively so they come to me directly.

When you connect with me and decide to work with me one to one, we take a deep dive into your womb space. We heal through every single chakra level, something I will go into later, peeling away the layers of stress, trauma, pain buried in your cellular memory of your womb space.

My clients may experience certain emotions and feelings within their womb, perhaps a heaviness or lightness, some see colors. Others may connect with memories and situations. Each client experiences their womb differently, depending on how their sensory system works.

My clients can normally pick up on some energies yet they find it harder to translate what it is they are sensing. This is why it takes practice and consistency to dig deeply into the buried energies within your womb. And this is where I help my clients the most because I help to translate those energies.

I can see energies visually, for example, I see a situation where the parents are arguing and the child feels so lost and lonely. I see relationship problems where your power has been taken away from you and it's literally eating away on the inside, building up more and more so that you're not in your feminine flow anymore. I often see what can be described as symbolic imagery which is not an exact situation but something that gives meaning and depth to the pain and trauma within.

You can also do this yourself with practice, tuning into your womb, understanding, listening. It is something that I've simply always been able to do and tuned into it more and more over the years. We can all tap into it if we allow ourselves to be open to the flow of energy.

My Five Steps to Womb Healing Technique works because I guide women to communicate with their wombs, releasing negative cellular memory caused by trauma, pain and stress, and reviving their pure, positive energy flow.

Ladies with irregular or blocked menstrual cycles are experiencing their cycles returning and becoming regular again. Others are seeing their cysts healing and disappearing. It is such a massive release when you're back into your natural flow and your quality of life returns.

When you understand the power behind energy flow and the power of your thoughts, you understand how healing works. All you need to decide is to take that step and consistently do that self work on yourself.

It's about being in tune with the flow of nature and the flow of inner energy. When something is out of balance, it causes imbalance inside of our bodies. Think how much of our body is made up of water and the element of water and how good you feel around natural, flowing water. You feel good.

This is what it's all about being in tune with nature. And, as I've talked about earlier, we are becoming more and more out of balance due to being so wrapped up in our busy modern world. No time to stop. Not grounding ourselves. We don't notice the world around us when we are constantly online.

It's time for you to connect with your natural flow. Being in balance with the natural elements of nature is the core of shamanic healing. Now how do you feel about the word shaman? It doesn't sound like something to be feared, simply, a deep wisdom and connectedness with nature that has been misunderstood and misinterpreted over the years.

Your Connection With the Natural Elements Check In Exercise

Before we proceed with the rest of the book, let's first check in with where you're at right now with your connectedness with nature.

Below, rate yourself on a scale from 1 - 5 on how accurate the statements are

- 1 means "I feel completely disconnected" and
- 5 means "I feel deeply connected"

Once you've rated yourself for each statement, total up your scores and then use the Answer Key to determine your next steps.

Check in Exercise	Self Rating
Water: Think for a moment about how you feel around water, perhaps a river or waves on a beach, lapping against the sand, or a stream trickling and gurgling. Close your eyes and think about your favorite natural type of water; hear it, smell it, taste it, touch it. How does it make you feel? How connected are you with water on a daily basis? Rate yourself in the right hand side column.	

Earth: Think about earth, walking bare feet around in the garden on the grass, or digging your feet into sand at the beach. Close your eyes and feel into the sensations - is the sand/grass wet or dry? Which do you prefer? How does it make you feel? How connected are you with earth on a daily basis? Rate yourself in the right hand side column.	
Air: Think about air, the different types of air; when you go out for a walk and you have a gentle breeze blowing on your face, is it warm or cold, what time of year is it? Or do you prefer a blowing wind that whistles around your house and completely refreshes you when you go out into it? Close your eyes and think about your favorite type of air; hear it, smell it, taste it, touch it. How does it make you feel? How connected are you with air on a daily basis? Rate yourself in the right hand side column.	

Fire: Think about fire; when do you like being around fire? Perhaps an open log fire, cozy and warm in the winter time or perhaps a raging bonfire outside, watching the sparks fly up into the sky? Close your eyes and think about how the energy of fire makes you feel, using your senses to feel, smell and hear it. How connected are you with fire on a daily basis? Rate yourself in the right hand side column.	

Understanding Your Score

First things first - what do you notice when looking at your self ratings? Are you more connected / disconnected with one to two elements? If so, this is already showing you where you are currently imbalanced.

0 - 8
Disconnection With Nature's Elements is Blocking Your Own Natural Flow

With a score this low you are probably already thinking "how can I get myself more connected?". Can you feel just how out of touch you are and how much your body needs this connection with the four elements? When we flow with nature, our inner energy flow is strengthened. After all, we came from nature.

Now that you have made this realization, think about how you can strengthen your connection with the elements. Walking around barefoot may not be easy if you live in the city or at winter time. Think about how you can connect with earthly energy in your own home; do you have many plants that you can tend to? If you are out for a walk, can you stop and place your hand on the trunk of a tree?

Notice the air you are breathing more. Light candles regularly. Make that trip to the river, lake or to the seafront, each time really noticing how you are feeling around each of these elements.

As you bring in more balance and connectedness with the four elements, continue to implement the Five Steps to Womb Healing Technique. Notice how your energy flow improves in general as you connect more with nature and with your womb.

9 - 13
Becoming More In Tune

You are feeling generally connected yet not as deeply as you would like. Perhaps one or two of the elements are very easy for you to connect with and you have less time for the others? Could you feel the imbalance in your body as you were imagining the four elements?

Now that you are more aware of this imbalance, you can think about how to bring in that balance. Perhaps writing Earth, Air, Fire, Water on the front of your journal to give yourself that small reminder to connect with all four.

As you become more in tune and balanced, you will feel the differences within your body. The more you build your confidence with womb connection, using the Five Steps to Womb Healing Technique, the more you will notice how your balance with the four elements supports you to create a harmonized flow in your body.

14 - 20
Bring That Energy Within

You are already very in tune. Just a little fine tuning will bring you a wonderful sense of harmony with all four elements. All you need to do now is to bring the energies into your womb.

My Five Steps to Womb Healing Technique will equip you with the know-how to communicate with your womb. Because you are so connected with the four elements you should find my techniques to be a complementary journey within.

You may be surprised when you realize you just weren't connecting deeply within your womb before...you have been doing so much in terms of stress release to help yourself but that all important womb connection has been missing.

It's time for you to deeply connect in with your womb. Feeling the energies within is like the missing piece of the puzzle for you. Once you tune in to the flow of communication from your womb, you will be able to understand the heavy energies behind your blockages and amplify your healing journey.

Perhaps one problem you may encounter is translating the energies behind your blockages once the communication flow is established. It may be frustrating that it takes time to understand when you have already come so far. You've got this and my 1:1 support is always there to help you to interpret and feel confident with your womb communication.

CHAPTER SIX

THE NUMBER ONE PROBLEM WITH SELF WOMB HEALING

"Trust and consistency are what bring you healing shifts."

- Vicki Renz

I love using self womb healing to connect with my womb. I love guiding you with my Five Steps Technique to connect with your womb.

But there is a problem with how women are going about their self womb healing which we shall explore here.

Many women have tried womb healing and been disappointed in their results. The specific reason for their disappointment is the topic of this chapter.

Put simply, just trying out womb healing on yourself a couple of times does not make any longer term sense.

Perhaps trying my technique out and then not believing in yourself so you put it to one side. Or you try it out and can't feel much in terms of womb communication so you give up. Many people view womb healing as something "woo woo" and may question you when you get excited and talk about it, this may deter you from continuing your womb healing techniques on yourself, doubting yourself and the technique.

Womb healing is a communication that takes place between you, your heart and your womb space. If you are completely new to it, it takes practice and will get better and clearer with time. If you just try it once and dismiss it because maybe you didn't feel anything the first time then try again!

With so many women getting amazing results I sincerely encourage you to pick up my techniques, try them again and keep on going.

If you find doubt is creeping in or you really don't feel like you are doing things right then I invite you to come and chat with me. Receive my personal guidance where you get to feel confident that you are "doing things right". I invite you to apply for a call to chat with me by following the link or scanning the code:

https://wombhealing.ohmymamabody.com/5stepstechnique-bookcall

When you connect in with your womb with my proven techniques, I know you will feel positive changes within your body. Break through blockages, challenges, stress, anxiety and reclaim your natural fertile flow.

Womb healing on its own is a powerful technique yet keeping that momentum, feeling great about yourself, trusting in yourself and in the process is one of the biggest problems around your healing journey. You will no doubt be faced with challenges and having days where you feel like throwing it all in, that's why I love to be your cheerleader so that you keep on going.

So many women want to know if they are doing it right. You feel so much assurance when sharing experiences, rather than doubting and giving it up instead of continuing.

There is an incredible power when women join together. It intensifies the healing. It strengthens you on your journey.

So If that's something you would like more support with, go ahead and book a call with me to get the support and energy you really need to keep you going, to keep you motivated and to get your womb healing energies flowing.

YOUR WOMB HEALING MOTIVATION - CHECK IN EXERCISE

Before we proceed with the rest of the book, let's first check in with where you're at right now with taking action.

Below, rate yourself on a scale from 1 - 5 on how accurate the statements are:

- 1 means “Not at all” and
- 5 means “Yes 100%”

Once you’ve rated yourself for each statement, total up your scores and then use the Answer Key to determine your next steps.

Womb Healing Motivation Check in Statement	Self Rating
I feel positive about trying womb healing and keen to create shifts in my womb energy	
I don’t care if others think that womb healing is “woo woo”, I want to try it out and see for myself	
I understand that I need to implement womb healing techniques daily to get the best results for myself	
I am determined to master womb connection	
If I feel like I am not getting results on my own I will seek personal guidance in order to make better progress	

Score 0 - 10
Feeling Unsure is Holding You Back

The bad news is that you are missing the motivation and consistency to be able to achieve effective shifts with your womb healing practice. You've probably realized this whilst you answered the questions.

The good news is that you can turn this around and really get into your womb healing. If others around you don't understand why you are trying womb healing, choose to surround yourself with like-minded people.

Consider how joining my Tribe could radically improve your approach to womb healing as you experience the positive flow of shifts first hand. Sometimes all it takes is to experience the benefit of initial energy shifts to spark your motivation.

Score 11 - 18
You're On Your Way to Making Good Progress

Is it more about finding the time to master womb healing and perhaps what others will think about you trying out something "woo woo"?

Go through the "Why Womb Healing Works" section to reassure yourself and to also have a founded explanation for anyone who may question you.

Remember, those closest to us are often the ones who will question us the most which leads us to feel uncertain.

Finding time for your womb healing will get easier as you begin to experience energetic shifts. Start by scheduling in basic daily womb connection upon waking and two to three twenty minute time slots for going through the five steps. That's just one hour a week to fit into your busy schedule.

As you experience the revival of your energy flow, you'll start to enjoy those twenty minute sessions and find yourself scheduling in more time for those transformational shifts.

Score 19 - 25
Your Determination Is on Fire

Your motivation and consistency will bring so much positive flow with the time you are dedicating to your womb healing. You know that you can master the techniques and create positive results for yourself.

For you, the biggest hurdle is to dig deep enough to work through the many layers of heavy energy. That's where my self-paced womb healing modules come in. You'll find deeper guidance through the ten chakra layers, helping you to discover and understand on all levels of your energy system.

Get ready to profoundly release and experience feeling revitalized confidence and inner strength as you rediscover the power of your true feminine flow.

CHAPTER SEVEN

THE PROBLEM OF NERVOUS STRESS

"Every day is a new opportunity to leave the stress behind and choose to start with positive flow."

- Vicki Renz

Each time you think about your struggles with your womb, you may feel an overwhelming feeling of nervousness and stress. You find it hard to stop that flow of thought in your head. Those thoughts that spin everything out of control to make you feel worse. You can feel it rising in your chest and constricting your throat, an underlying fear of "what if it turns into something else?". "What if I will never be fertile?". "What if I can never have babies?". "What if my partner leaves me?".

These fears, some of them are so irrational yet they are building up more stress. Stress stores up inside of us over time. Everyday stress can increase our struggles. Struggles in our reproductive system due to Cortisol.

It is scientifically proven that stress releases a hormone called Cortisol which can interrupt the messages between our brain and our reproductive system. Cortisol can stop women from ovulating. It can put our reproductive hormones completely out of balance.

This may show up as irregular cycles, struggles trying to conceive or blockages in our womb space. When we are not in our regular flow, we feel completely disconnected and out of balance.

Finding balance, finding your flow and being in tune with your inner song: this is the key to changing the energies inside of you, for allowing yourself to release. Your fear, your panic, the constant stream of thoughts in your subconscious may feel like they are blocking you right now.

When you break through what seems at the moment to be a solid barrier, you will break through this because I know you can, you automatically start reducing the levels of Cortisol in your body. You begin to take back control of your thoughts which means you're back in control of your stress levels. You gradually turn things around and find your flow.

The biggest problem is being able to break through that barrier. Having the right techniques to help you get through with consistency and motivation. Feeling courage to release, allowing and trusting in your healing journey.

So many women who book their initial call with me for an introduction to womb healing are in such a state of stress. During our first conversation, they feel safe and held in my space and start opening up and having a heart to heart. They feel they can relax and let go by having someone who understands them and holds them and often the tears flow.

They allow that barrier to start breaking down as they start to release some of their stress, tension and nervousness that they have been holding on to for so long. I hold them in a trusting space. Being held they know that it is possible to release, they start to feel that their healing journey is beginning and that it's okay to let go and start feeling good.

On the other side of that barrier, it is possible to be like a strong, fulfilled, powerful, glowing woman. In just a few weeks she will be looking back and seeing how far she has come, how much she has released and just how good she is feeling.

I invite you to put yourself in that place. To visualize that future version of yourself in six months from now. That version of you with your cleansed womb. Clearly see and feel yourself in that place where there is no more fear or stress because you are confidently using the Five Steps to Womb Healing Technique.

Every single day you're healing and feeling wonderful. You have found your flow. You are so in tune with your inner self, your feminine core. You've let go of the constrictions that were tightening up your body. Your body feels light and free. You're starting to feel good about socializing again. You are getting back that life of yours.

This is what can happen when you realize that it is simply a case of putting in the practice consistently, shifting your heavy, negative energies. The better you get at it, the faster you will get back your quality of life.

Celebrate yourself, to see far you've come already by getting this far by reading this far.

Ask yourself these questions:

- ▲ How long is it going to take me to get to that place of healing?
- ▲ How much do I desire to get to that place?
- ▲ How much time am I willing to put into self care to reach that place?
- ▲ What happens when I feel challenged to keep on? Do I give up or continue?
- ▲ What is my goal for six months from now?

Future Visualization Exercise - Your 6 Month Goals

This is an embodied journaling exercise. The key to manifesting your goals is to feel the emotions of reaching your goals; imagining with all of your senses that you have already reached your goal.

Taking out your journal, ask yourself the following questions and write down your answers and thoughts:

- ▲ What are my goals for my womb 6 months from now?
- ▲ How does my womb feel 6 months from now?

- ▲ How do I feel 6 months from now?
- ▲ What does my life look like now that I have achieved these goals?

  - Here, start with "it is 6 months from now (write down the month) and I am ..." describe in detail where you are, what you are doing, who you are with, what you are wearing, what you are eating.
  - Bring in all of your senses to make this feel as real as possible.

- ▲ How am I celebrating myself now that I have reached these goals?

This is a great exercise to journal about daily or as regularly as you can, to program your subconscious to believe in yourself. It works so well and is incredibly uplifting.

Really feel into your visualization like everything is already happening. Repeat as often as you can.

CHAPTER EIGHT

WHAT HAPPENS IF YOUR WOMB REMAINS BLOCKED?

"We are blessed with a womb that regularly releases, so celebrate your flow, it is a gift (not a curse)."

– Vicki Renz

Let's take something similar so that you can relate to what I am about to describe. Think about it this way; if you go to the dentist because you are experiencing a toothache, your dentist will check, diagnose you and advise you on the best way forward.

For example, if you have sore gums because you have a buildup of plaque, your dentist will most likely advise a thorough clean and carry this out so your symptoms don't get worse.

It is then up to you to keep your teeth clean by regular brushing and flossing. If you don't keep this up, you will end up in the same situation again.

Now thinking about your womb; you know you have physical blockages or are experiencing imbalance because your doctor has given you a diagnosis. Perhaps you have been advised to take painkillers, birth control pills, to watch your diet, take exercise, or in more severe cases you are facing the possibility of surgery to physically remove your blockages.

You know how this is making you feel; frustrated, self-conscious, anxious and stressed, to name but a few. You also know, from what you have read so far, that the medical side is not going to solve the energetic root cause of your blockages.

Over time, you may become more frustrated and further disconnected from your womb, negative, heavy energy will continue to build up on the inside leading to further blockages and raised stress.

As already discussed, stress leads to Cortisol being released which can directly impact your reproductive system, causing more imbalance. All in all, you become stuck in a vicious cycle of build up by not taking action to connect with your womb energy.

I invite you to ask yourself what your life will look like 6 months from now if nothing changes and your symptoms and blockages remain.

- ▲ How will you be feeling?
- ▲ What will your daily life look like?

Now ask yourself:

- What is it worth to me to invest time in my womb healing? Hint: refer to your 6 month goals from the previous chapter.

With that in mind, are you ready to start your womb healing journey?

PART TWO

THE FIVE STEPS TECHNIQUE

CHAPTER NINE

INTRODUCING THE 5 STEPS TECHNIQUE TO HEALING YOUR WOMB

My five steps to womb healing technique is a proven technique that guides you to deeply connect with your womb and understand the energies behind your blockages so that you can heal and release them.

Your womb is a vessel of creation, like your second heart. We can feel emotions in our heart so easily; you know the terms “aching heart”, “heavy heart”, yet most of us can't feel into our womb in the same way.

We have become so distanced from our wombs. Yet it is simply an art of remembering how to connect again, discover and understand the emotions, experiences, trauma and pain that you're holding on within your womb that is being presented as imbalance and physical blockages, upsetting your natural feminine flow.

Your inner balance is out of sync due to not releasing deep stress and trauma. It has built up over time and now your womb is crying out for you to take notice of her.

The good news is that you are taking notice because you're here reading my Five Steps to Womb Healing Technique. As well as learning how to connect with the heavy energies that are creating your womb blockages and healing them. In doing this, you'll also be getting rid of feelings of inadequacy, low self worth, growing in confidence and inner strength.

These five steps are so powerful on many levels in your life. As you get your energy back and feel great about yourself, your confidence strengthens. You start to flow fully in your feminine power, your quality of life returns. You feel great showing up and socializing.

The five steps are Connect, Discover, Understand, Heal and Release. I'll be guiding you through each one of the steps with an explanation and exercise so that you can feel your energy flow by yourself and equip yourself with the techniques to heal your womb.

These steps can be repeated daily as you get more familiar with your womb and dig deeper into your blockages.

Womb healing is a gradual process, like peeling off the layers of an onion. Ask any healer, they will tell you that they themselves are constantly healing. This is why being consistent is key to your progress.

Our lives here on Earth are of a cyclical nature; growth, learning, shedding, repeat. We live in a continuous cycle of growth, even if we do sometimes feel stuck, eventually we come out on the other side.

Have you noticed this in your life? A challenge shows itself, at first you don't know how to get through it, but then the solution comes. Sometimes you don't even realize you've got to the other side of the challenge until you find yourself thinking back a few months later.

One of the biggest obstacles we face is not to get stuck in the challenge, feeling that the world is against us. Sometimes we really need to push and motivate ourselves to get to the other side of our challenges. It may be hard to do this on our own, which is when we call upon a Guide, someone who has been there and made it through themselves.

My 1:1 clients reach out to me because they know they need that extra, personal guidance and support. They are familiar with my fertility story, they've watched my YouTube videos, they trust me and know that I completely understand them and hold the space for them. I guide and motivate them to heal through their challenges using my techniques and always being that listener and cheerleader by their side.

The Healing Process

It is important to remember that healing is a gradual process. Your womb has communicated and shared some of what she is holding on to with you. You will find that each time you go through the Discover and Understand Steps, more will be revealed and communicated to you.

The layers of healing go very deep. In fact, when I work one to one with my ladies, we work through each chakra level as well as directly with the areas of blockage in their womb. Healing at each chakra level includes the seven chakras in our body and the 3 upper chakras; your Higher Self, your Universal and your Divine Gateway chakras. You may choose to take your healing to the next level with my self study modules which I talk about later on in this book.

You can think about healing taking place at a physical and non physical body level. We are surrounded by energy and we have our own energy field. You can recognize energy fields, for example when someone walks into a room and their energy lights up the place, or brings it down. The human body emits enough energy to power a lightbulb. We can't see this but we know it's there when we get static shocks.

So we have a flow of energy going in and out of our body as well as circulating within. In healing terms, energies of trauma and stress first take place within our outer energy field. Depending on the level of trauma and stress experienced, this could be left in our outer energy field or it could get stronger and eventually manifest physically within our body.

This is where shamanic healing supports healing to go to the next level because the technique picks up on energy flow within the body and without the body.

Healing at the level of the 3 upper chakras often reveals trauma and stress passed down through generations, past life experiences and contracts or even interdimensional attachments. This is why womb healing requires an open mind and consistency; there are many layers to heal through.

I personally work on myself every single day; using morning womb connection, breathwork techniques and embodied journaling techniques to release my everyday stress. Often I experience an almost overwhelming feeling of negativity or something just not sitting right with my energy. I am always grateful for these signs as it shows me that there is something in my energy field to be shifted. Something new is showing itself and is ready to be shifted and healed.

That's how we grow and evolve as human beings; we are in a state of constant flow and change.

That’s why it’s important to keep on going with your womb healing. Don't be surprised when new things come up for you.

CHAPTER TEN

THE FIVE STEPS TECHNIQUE EXERCISES

Preparing for Your Womb Healing

1. Connect with nature:

It is great if you can firstly spend some time in nature. Find time for calm and peace away from the busy every day. Ground yourself and connect with the four elements. Use whatever you have that is practical and close by; a forest, trees, a green area, water. Take yourself outside. Walk around, sit and breathe, connecting and listening in to the flow of nature all around you.

2. Find a suitable space:

To go through the womb healing steps, find a space where you can feel comfortable, relaxed and knowing that you can't be disturbed by anyone. You can choose to either sit or lie down. If lying down, it is good to prop your head up well, otherwise you may find that you fall asleep! That can happen when you are doing deep inner work.

Perhaps you'd like to wear headphones or earplugs so that you don't get distracted by any external noises. Ensure that you can really be in your space and able to tune into your inner flow.

3. Something to drink:

Have something to drink close by. It's always great to top your body up with water after any healing session.

4. Writing things down:

Keep a pen and paper / journal nearby so that you can write down your thoughts and experiences after each self womb healing session. It's always really great to keep note of the communication flow with your womb; what came up and the healing experience. You can look back at your healing progress over time and see how far you've come.

It is natural that your mind will try to jump in and question you as you go through these exercises. When you use your senses to connect with your womb, you may find your mind jumps in and questions if you are doing it right or if you are even making things up, or your mind may start to wander. When this happens, gently tell your mind that these thoughts can be left to one side for now, you can come back to them later because right now you would like to concentrate on your womb.

This is often a massive reason why ladies join my Tribe so that they have continual support and personal guidance. It helps them to feel confidence in their womb healing and with my guidance they experience healing and release in a supportive space rather than on their own. They find it a lot easier to concentrate when being guided, rather than taking themselves through the steps.

Step One - Connect

Now that you've got your comfortable place and have gone through the preparation points, you can start your womb healing.

There are two levels to womb connection; the first level is to sense and acknowledge your womb. This is something you can easily do on a daily basis. The second level is to travel into your womb with your inner vision. Traveling into your womb may seem strange at first and you may find yourself resisting and questioning yourself. Take a few deep breaths and concentrate on the exercise, following my guide step by step.

The more connected you become with your womb, the better you will be able to sense her during your everyday life. The more in tune you are with what your womb is communicating to you, the greater you will be able to find your inner balance and strength.

Exercise One - Connecting Your Heart and Your Womb

This is an exercise which you can practice daily. I love to do this upon waking, acknowledging my womb and connecting deeply with my inner feminine flow. When you are new to this exercise, it helps to journal about your experiences. Over time, you can read back on your progress in connecting and communicating with your womb, showing you how far you have come.

- ▲ Start by placing one hand over your heart and one hand over your womb.
- ▲ Breathe in and out through your nose, noticing how your breath rises and falls in your chest.
- ▲ Notice if you are taking shallow breaths and changing this by taking deeper breaths which reach into your stomach as well, slowing down your breathing.
- ▲ Take your focus to your heart. Notice your heart beating. Feel your heart energy, noticing what it feels like as you breathe into your heart.
- ▲ Now start thinking about a situation where you were really happy. Where were you then? Were you with anyone else? What were you wearing?
- ▲ Can you relive the moment and feel the happy energy of that moment in your heart?
- ▲ Notice how your energy shifts to happiness within your heart.
- ▲ Now visualize this energy flowing down into your womb. Concentrate on sending your loving heart energy down into your womb. You may like to

visualize a flow of white or pink light, connecting between your heart and your womb.

- ▲ Feel your womb gratefully receiving your love.
- ▲ Notice what that feels like to have this connection with your womb and how she responds as she receives your happy energy flow.
- ▲ Become aware of any feelings, sensations or emotions that your womb may communicate with you at this stage.
- ▲ Continue to make this beautiful heart-womb connection until you feel like you have filled every single cell in your womb with loving energy.
- ▲ Notice how it feels for you to be deeply connected with your feminine core.
- ▲ When you are ready and feel like you have made a connection and felt some communication in the form of feelings, sensations and/or emotions.
- ▲ When you are ready, open your eyes, noticing how that feels within your body.
- ▲ Take some time to journal about what you experienced.

Did you notice how much you were in your body rather than in your mind, once you brought in the feeling of happy energy flow and focusing on your heart and your womb?

Exercise Two - Traveling to Your Womb With Your Inner Vision

You can choose to do this exercise either as a continuation of Exercise One or separately. Keep an open mind and go with the visualizations. This is an extremely effective technique once you have mastered it.

- ▲ To begin with, place one hand over your heart and one hand over your womb, breathing gently into your body, becoming aware of the feelings and sensations inside of your body.
- ▲ As you breathe and connect in with your inner flow, set the intention for yourself to connect and communicate with your womb.
- ▲ Take your focus to your third eye (slightly above and between your eyebrows), feel the focus of your energy in that area, visualizing a small vortex, dark blue in color, that spins slowly clockwise outwards from your third eye
- ▲ Stay with that visual for a good minute or two, keeping your mind focused on the visual.
- ▲ Now I invite you to visualize a small version of yourself standing in that vortex. This version of you is small enough to travel down inside of your body.
- ▲ Visualize this small you walking towards your third eye and naturally stepping inside of your head and dropping down into your throat.

- ▲ This small version of you gently travels further down into your body; into the top of your chest, your heart space, gradually dropping further through your diaphragm and eventually arriving at your womb.
- ▲ When the small version of you arrives at your womb, simply step into your womb.
- ▲ Once inside your womb, allow yourself time to take everything in with all of your senses.
- ▲ From where that small version of you is standing, take a look around, above and below. Gently breathing and immersing yourself in the experience of connecting with your womb from within.
- ▲ When you are feeling ready to travel back up out of your womb, firstly thank your womb for sharing with you.
- ▲ Now simply step back out of your womb and start gradually traveling back up through your body, going the same way you did on the way down to your womb.
- ▲ Feel yourself reaching your third eye and stepping back into the dark blue vortex.
- ▲ Visualize that small version of you gradually growing back to your normal size and merging back with your body.
- ▲ Notice your hand over your heart and your other hand over your womb.

- Feel your breath rising and falling and your heart beating as you ground back into your body.
- Now place your hands palm and palm together, gently rubbing them to create a little warmth. This helps you to ground back into your body.
- Gradually open your eyes and have a stretch. Take a sip of water.
- Pick up your journal and write down your experience.

Now that you know how to journey into your body and connect with your womb from within, you are ready to go to the next steps.

Step Two - Discover

This phase is about discovering your womb from the inside. Use your senses to experience your womb. You may find that you question yourself if what you are sensing is for real or perhaps you are making it up. Your experience will be very individual, depending on what type of sensory person you are. My best advice to you is to trust in the process.

Firstly, start with Connect Exercise Two so that you are already within your womb.

- From inside your womb, just take a moment to look around. Feel and notice all of your senses as you take in your womb space.
- Notice any darker areas or lighter areas.

- What is the predominant color of your womb? Do you notice several colors?
- Do you feel like it is a welcoming space?
- Are you picking up on any emotions?
- How do you feel standing inside your womb?
- Having a look around, do you notice areas which are looking more dense or blocked?
- Take your time to explore around your womb, paying attention to areas which you sense to be blocked.
- You can walk over to these areas and explore them close up. Have a look over them to see how it feels to view them from close up. Notice what these areas look like - the shape, size, color and if you pick up on any feelings, energies or emotions.
- Do these areas appear to be still or do they seem to shift, move or even change color?
- Focus in gradually, taking in as much detail as you can, taking time to observe and sense.
- What does it feel like to be observing your womb from within?
- At this stage, do not ask any questions, simply sense and observe.

You may find this phase to be emotional as your womb starts to reveal the heaviness that you are holding on to within. Take your time and keep on going. If you need to take a break and write things down, follow your instinct and come back to the Discover stage again once you have written things down and feel more settled.

You can choose to continue on to the Understand phase from here or to travel back up out of your womb and take notes.

Step Three - Understand

Firstly, start with Connect Exercise Two and Understand steps.

Take your time to really understand what it is that your womb is communicating with you and showing you during this phase of womb healing. You are connecting deeply with your cellular memory.

If you find yourself getting distracted, concentrate on your breathing for a few moments and then connect back in with your womb. Try not to force yourself. It's best to have a clear mind and feel relaxed to experience a clear communication.

Understanding - Exercise One

- ▲ That little version of you walks over to an area you have observed to be more dense or blocked.
- ▲ Getting close enough to this area, place a hand gently on the area, connecting directly with it.
- ▲ Allow a communication to flow between this area of your womb and yourself.

- ▲ Concentrate on sensing what is being shown and revealed to you from within.
- ▲ As the communication flows, ask your womb to show you what you are burying within.
- ▲ Visualize that this area of your womb can show you a small movie screen which can play events back to you. Concentrate on what is being shown to you.
- ▲ When you feel like you have sensed enough communication, gradually make your way back out of your womb, thanking your womb for the connection.

Understanding - Exercise Two - Digging Deeper

Once you have communicated with your womb a few times and feel confident with the flow of communication you are receiving, it's time to dig deeper to get more information. The key to womb healing is to get to the root cause of the energies behind your blockages, accessing your cellular memory and releasing any negativity.

When digging deeper, you can choose whether to ask your womb out loud or to ask in your head, whichever is more comfortable or feels right for you. Allow your womb time to respond to one question at a time. It may take a few goes to get to this next level of information, so keep an open and calm mind.

You're asking some very basic questions to get more clarity and as you do this, concentrate, allow that flow and again, don't push it. If little information comes at this stage, that's okay. You can come back to this, don't push it if it's not quite ready yet.

- ▲ Following on from Understand Exercise One, gradually dig deeper by asking the following questions:
    - Can you give me more signs or information so that I understand you better?
    - What am I holding on to that is causing my blockages?
    - What is it that you are showing to me?
- ▲ When you feel you have received a good flow of communication you can continue to dig deeper:
    - Why is this causing me stress?
    - Why are you blocking my womb?
- ▲ Breathe gently into the flow of communication and feel like you can look deeply into the area which is blocked, feeling open to receiving information.
- ▲ At this stage you should be starting to pick up on memories, emotions and feelings that are more specific and that you can relate to.
- ▲ When you feel like you've received enough information, thank your womb for the communication and connection.

You can choose if you'd like to travel back up out of your womb and spend time journaling about what you have experienced. It's good to write things down so that your experiences stay clear in your mind.

Journaling in itself is very healing as you write your feelings and emotions down.

Or you can continue to stay in your womb and go to the next phase of healing the memories, feelings and emotions that you have discovered and started to understand the negative energies that you are holding on to.

Know that the more you practice, the more you are going to be able to connect with your womb and let that communication flow. You've probably got more of an idea of what kind of sensory person you are now from the Understand phase.

Were you able to let go and be open to a flow of communication from your womb? Did you sense heaviness or lightness, see dark and light or perhaps different colors? How did the movie screen work for you? Could you receive visuals of events in your life past and present? Or perhaps events that weren't familiar to you at all?

However you experienced your journey of discovery and understanding, it is perfectly fine. The more you allow and trust the flow, the more you will sense as you get used to connecting with the information you're receiving from your womb

Many women love joining my Tribe to help them to open up more to their communication flow with their womb because they find themselves feeling unsure and feel they need guidance.

If you are feeling like this, come and join my Tribe. Surround yourself with others in the same space as you, understand what you're discovering inside of your womb. Gain confidence so that you can get to the root cause and to heal deeply, releasing your blockages that have been holding you back for so long.

Step Four - Heal

For your healing to be most effective, I recommend going into each topic (that you have found during the Discover Step) one at a time. That emotion, memory or feeling, approach them one by one, knowing that your healing is a journey of self discovery and release.

Healing Exercise One

Start with the previous exercises. If you have taken a break after the Understand step, start with the Connection to bring yourself into your womb.

- Set your intention at this stage for healing to take place, concentrating on that smaller version of yourself inside of your womb.
- Connect with that emotion, memory or experience that your blockage has been showing you.

- Breathe and take time to sense into your blockage. As you are connecting in, know that you're connecting in as your present adult self. You've grown so much since this event, experience or emotion.

- Looking at this energy now feeling love and compassion in your heart, send love and compassion into the energy of the trauma and the stress holding it.

- Remember, you are unable to undo the experience from happening but you can change the energy being held inside to that of love and forgiveness for yourself and for others involved.

- Take your time to allow this flow of love and forgiveness to really be felt within your blockage.

- Notice if you can sense your blockage receiving this energy and if you can sense any release taking place.

- If there is something you would like to communicate to yourself or to others involved, allow those words to flow. Perhaps you are giving yourself the love you needed at the time, perhaps you are forgiving others involved. It is important to do this from a place of love in order to allow the energy to heal, to help it feel better. Forgiveness is the ultimate healing.

- Deeply concentrate on this flow until you sense that your blockage is receiving your healing. Depending on how you are sensing your blockage you may notice changes such as lightness, changes in color or density, emotions lightening or feeling more at ease.

- When you feel good about the healing flow, that enough has flowed, thank your womb for this healing experience and gradually travel back.

- Take time to journal about your experience.

You may feel you are struggling with the healing exercises; it can be hard to let go of feelings of hurt, anger or resentment. Go gently on yourself. Work on the situation little by little to bring in the forgiveness and love it needs. You can realize how much this is blocking you when it is harder to let go of.

I understand that the healing process can be very deep and you may prefer to have more guidance. My Womb Vitality online guided modules, which I discuss later on in this book, accompany you on your womb healing journey, bringing you extra confidence and support with the Five Steps Technique.

Step Five - Release

Once you have felt into the healing, forgiveness and love around the energies that you are holding on to in your womb, it's time to fully release them from your womb space.

This is an exercise to separate energetic cords between yourself, your womb and others. You may feel like your pain and emotion is still very much attached to an individual or event and it is pulling on your energy. Going through the Healing Exercise, you probably felt your energy draining as you connected in.

Follow these steps to create healthy boundaries and disconnect any energetic cords of energy so that you can get back your full flow of energy, feeling revitalized. You will be able to feel just how much those energetic cords have been affecting your everyday life once you have released them.

Start with the previous exercises. If you have taken a break after the Healing step, start with the Connection to bring yourself into your womb.

- ▲ Visualize a protective light surrounding your whole womb. Imagine the light that is associated with angels and the halo shining.
- ▲ Feel the protective strength of this light around your womb.
- ▲ Now visualize the event, person or people associated with your blockage. See them at what feels like a safe distance apart from you so that your boundaries are not invaded.
- ▲ Visualize protective light surrounding the event, person or each person.
- ▲ Now notice any cords of energy attaching yourself to the event, person or people. There may be one or many cords. The cords could be different thicknesses. Take your time to become aware of all of them.

- Your next step is to release these cords by dissolving them. You can do this by sending love along the cords. You could visualize this as sending a white light along the cords, starting from yourself and traveling along the cord to the event, person or people.
- Take your time, going from one cord to the next. You may find that some cords are thicker and tougher than others. Notice the cords gradually dissolving and disappearing as you send white light along them.
- When you feel confident that all of the cords have been dissolved, spend a moment to reinforce the protective energy surrounding your womb, focusing on the white light.
- Now observe the event, person or people. See the situation surrounded in its own energy. Gradually visualize them distancing themselves from you, creating clear boundaries for yourself, knowing that this situation is no longer serving you and you have healed all energetic attachments with love.
- Breathe in the feeling of standing in your reinforced energetic boundary. Notice how you are feeling.
- As you create distance between yourself and the situation, imagine it being sent off to a place of love, protection and nourishment. Letting it distance further and further away from you, almost

like it's drifting off like a cloud into the sky and dissolving. Notice it completely dissolving.

- ▲ Come back to focus on your own energy field breathing in that new found strength and energy.
- ▲ When you are ready, thank your womb for this releasing experience and gradually travel back.
- ▲ Take time to journal about your experience. Write down how it feels to have let go of that situation.

Note: energetic cords may find their way back to you and attach themselves again, especially at the beginning of your healing journey. I recommend going through this exercise regularly to check yourself for any cord attachments.

PART THREE

CONTINUING FORWARD

Congratulations on completing the Five Steps to Womb Healing. I know it takes effort and commitment to yourself to work through the steps. How are you feeling? Many women will feel what can only be described as lightness following the releasing stage.

Remember, the rewards from investing time in your womb healing are plentiful. After consistently practicing womb healing, women who have irregular or missed periods find that their periods return and they become regular with more womb healing practice. Ladies are feeling pain relief, going for scans and finding their blockages have reduced or disappeared. Those trying to conceive get their positive test.

The possibilities are incredible as you continue to practice womb healing consistently on yourself.

CHAPTER ELEVEN

YOUR POSITIVE SHIFTS

"I choose to connect, flow and glow."

- Vicki Renz

Continue going through the steps, working on your womb healing and opening yourself up to your fully flowing and glowing inner feminine self:

- As you release energies behind your blockages, you're freeing up your womb space.
- You are releasing buried anxiety, trauma and everyday stress.
- You're reducing the stress levels in your body which means the communication flow between your brain and your reproductive system improves.
- Messages can flow and gradually your hormones find balance.

- ▲ As you regulate and balance, you feel inner strength and confidence.
- ▲ By reducing buried stress, Cortisol levels are reduced which leads to a healthier nervous and immune system.
- ▲ You are more in touch with your feminine flow and connected with your feminine core.
- ▲ You are clearing out old energies and patterns which have been holding you back and blocking you on so many levels in your life. You will be feeling that you can express your true self and feel so confident in doing so.
- ▲ You feel strengthened and powerful as you release heavy energies from your body.
- ▲ You start to fall in love with your incredible womb and feel the joyful energy of life as you rediscover your passions.
- ▲ You are moving towards constant positive flow. Soon you will be like a positivity magnet as your energy is cleansed from the inside out as you consistently practice womb healing on a daily basis.

CHAPTER TWELVE

DAILY ROUTINE FOR POSITIVE WOMB ENERGY FLOW

"Each small exercise will make a difference overall, find those bursts of time and feel the changes."

- Vicki Renz

To get the most out of your womb healing it is crucial that you set yourself up a daily routine. Here are my recommendations for you to incorporate into your day for a positive womb healing experience:

Waking Up Exercise

The first few seconds when you wake up are absolutely vital for determining your day ahead. Focus on your routine before you start thinking about the day ahead and everything you have to do.

This is your time to connect in with your body, your inner flow and who you are. I recommend you set yourself the intention to connect in with your womb each and every morning as the first thing you do.

Level One

Go through this routine as soon as you wake up.

- ▲ Place one hand over your heart and the other hand over your womb.
- ▲ Focus on breathing and connecting with your heart and your womb.
- ▲ Feel love flowing inside your body, between your heart and your womb.
- ▲ Breathe in and out five times.
- ▲ This creates a positive flow from your feminine core which will stay with you throughout your day ahead.

Level Two

You can choose to add to this routine, to make it even more powerful for your day ahead.

- ▲ Think about three positive statements about your life, saying them to yourself in your head. For example, “I'm so grateful for my comfortable bed”. “I'm so grateful for the birds that are singing in the garden”. “I am celebrating myself for the inner work that I'm doing on myself". "I'm so grateful to be alive this morning".

- You may continue and say five to ten positivity statements to yourself.

Through these statements you are programming your energy flow to be in a positive state of flow. When you start off in this positive flow, it continues throughout the day.

Of course during the day you're going to encounter external pressures and stresses which may push you off that positive flow. My tip for you is, when you get a chance, take a moment to go back into your heart-womb connection and back into that feeling you had first thing in the morning to reset your energy flow into the positive.

Level Three

To further strengthen this routine you can add intentions:

- Set yourself three intentions for your day ahead. These intentions can be things you intend to do or how you're going to feel during the day. For example "Today I intend to be in my positive flow all day". "Today, I choose positivity". "Today I choose to feel motivated and get my to do list done".

You can develop this in your own way. Perhaps starting off with the first step of the routine and gradually building on it. All in all you only need two to three minutes to set off your day in a positive flow. You will see the difference after you've done this for two to three days. Take note, look back on yourself, noticing that amazing difference in yourself.

Womb Healing Routine

Your next step is including womb healing into your daily or weekly routine. I recommend womb healing at least three times a week when you are starting out.

At this initial stage of connecting in with your womb, you require a lot of focus at the Discover and Understand steps. You need to be gentle and patient with the steps as you get more confident with your communication flow, allowing it to gradually build and become more clear for you.

I recommend making a date with yourself. I like to set an appointment with myself in my calendar with a reminder set. Take 20 minutes each day or every three days, however that fits into your current schedule. Make sure you honor that time.

Embodied Journaling Routine

Journaling is a very powerful technique when done regularly and with embodiment. You can keep journaling time down to just five minutes a day.

Basic Journaling:

- ▲ Write down three positive statements about yourself.
- ▲ Set three intentions for your day ahead or the day tomorrow (depending on the time of day you are journaling).
- ▲ Celebrating yourself for your achievements from the previous day.

Embodied Future-paced Journaling

- ▲ Future paced journaling is setting yourself a clear vision of what your life looks like in three /six / nine / twelve months from now (you decide on the time interval) and bringing the reality of how that feels into the present moment.
- ▲ Set yourself clear goals of where you would like to be by your chosen interval of time.
- ▲ Writing these goals down, start to visualize yourself already having achieved these goals.
- ▲ For example, imagine that today is already three months from now and you've achieved the goals you set out for yourself in your vision. How does that feel? What does it look like? What are you doing? Make that really present and real and use your senses to really feel this inside of your body. Write down the answers to these questions down and repeat this every single day.

- This is work at a subconscious level where you are training your brain to believe and trust in yourself and your way forward. The key is to already feel from within yourself that your goals have manifested. It is a very encouraging and motivating exercise.

CHAPTER THIRTEEN

HOW TO RELEASE QUICKLY

"Everything is possible when you are in the energy of self belief."

- Vicki Renz

You feel completely motivated and determined to release those blockages in your womb quickly? My advice to you is to put your daily routine into place and be consistent. Dedicate at least twenty minutes of womb healing time to yourself every single day.

Dive deeper and deeper into peeling away the layers of buried stress and trauma in your womb. That way you are going to achieve a faster healing.

If you feel frustrated and stuck at any point because you really want to achieve a fast healing yet, you're finding it difficult to get through the first steps of Discover and Understand, reach out and apply for a call with me for personal guidance and to discuss supportive options I have available for you.

Follow the link or scan the code:

https://wombhealing.ohmymamabody.com/5stepstechnique-bookcall

The Thing with Energy Flow

It is important to understand the thing with energy flow for your ongoing motivation and confidence. You can compare energy flow to the waves on the beach; energy flows, it comes and goes.

Picturing waves on the beach; some waves flow fast and reach a long way up the shore, gently flowing back or dissolving into the sand. Then there are smaller waves that lap at the shore and don't make it so far in. Then another surge of bigger waves that come in and make their way really far up the shore and as they pull back out into the sea, they clean the pebbles and stones on the beach.

Liken that imagery of waves to your womb healing. There are going to be times when you make massive steps forward, you uncover a massive blockage, you understand the energies at play and you feel a massive shift as you heal and release. Your life transforms and takes you to your next level.

Then maybe the next few times when you're working on your womb healing it may be harder to connect or focus. The blockages that you go into may seem really superficial, small and the shifts you experience are only small, just like those smaller waves.

Smaller waves will add up into a bigger wave over time. And remember, a bigger wave will be coming again soon. So it's important to keep working on yourself, keeping your motivation going. Remind yourself of the bigger picture.

This is why your journaling is so important. When you actively maintain your focus on that vision for yourself in the next three months (or whichever time interval you have chosen), you keep your momentum going. Shifts are gradual and it's only when you look back on yourself a few weeks later that you can really see just how far you've come.

PART FOUR

CONCLUSION

CHAPTER FOURTEEN

HOW TO GET MORE HELP

> *"I always wanted to do things on my own, until I experienced the leap of growth by having a caring teacher by my side."*
>
> *- Vicki Renz*

I've included a few extra resources for you to access as a reader of this Five Steps Technique Guide. It's a "thank you" to you and also because there isn't enough room to write everything in this book which is intended to be short and to the point so that you can achieve healing results fast.

The links below will take you to privately hosted videos where you can access the additional training.

Also, I've included information and a link on how I can help you with every step of your Five Steps to Womb Healing. I have multiple offerings, from DIY online modules to a deep, personal 1:1 guidance program. For more information, please see the details below.

Womb Healing Mastery Workshop

My most loved workshop. In this workshop I guide you through the first three steps of my Five Steps Technique so that you gain confidence with connecting in with your womb. I also include an embodied journaling and a gentle breathwork technique. Great for getting closely connected with your body and feeling the energy of my womb healing techniques.

Follow the link or scan the QR code:

https://wombhealing.ohmymamabody.com/5stepstechnique-bonuses

Womb Flow Revival Meditation

Let's get you communicating with your womb and feeling deeply connected with your inner feminine. This 15 minute meditation guides you to refresh the energy in your womb space, helping it to become unstuck so that you release blockages.

Plus you'll be feeling refreshed and revived after taking this short time out of your busy life, giving you renewed energy flow to continue with your day ahead.

Follow the link or scan the QR code:

https://wombhealing.ohmymamabody.com/5stepstechnique-bonuses

Protection for Electro Smog – What I Like to Use

We are surrounded my electro-magnetic frequencies in our home; computers, phones, tablets, WiFi...you name it! You may hear buzzing or often feel drained (a good reason to regularly connect with the elements).

I also like to use stickers which are designed to neutralize these frequencies by sticking them on my electronic devices.

Follow the link or scan the QR code to learn more:

Balanced Life Energy Stickers

Work With Me To Accelerate Your Womb Healing

If you loved what you read in this book and would like more personal guidance, support and motivation on your womb healing journey, I have a range of options for you:

Womb Healing - Learn Womb Communication Facebook Group

Come and join my free group on Facebook. Feel inspired and supported with regular updates from myself, messages and techniques.

Follow the link or scan the QR code:

https://www.facebook.com/groups/wombhealingfertility/

WOMMB (Women's Oh My Mama Body) Tribe

Ladies love the regular techniques and motivation that I guide them with in my Tribe. It's so much easier for them to join a guided group session rather than struggling on their own. You'll love the community spirit and feel held and understood.

It's your place to receive that extra boost and inspiration to take your womb healing to the next level. Ladies in the Tribe experience powerful shifts simply from making the bold decision to invest in themselves.

What you get in the Tribe:

- Guided embodied journaling for daily confidence in yourself and your vision
- Guided breathwork to release blockages

- Channeled New Moon Womb Healing for deep healing and Goddess guidance
- Q&A Sessions
- Group chats

Follow the link or scan the QR code:

https://wombhealing.ohmymamabody.com/5stepstechnique-joinwommbtribe

Womb Vitality Self Study Modules

You would like to feel more confident with your womb healing. You have felt some shifts as you went through the Five Steps Technique and would like more guidance and support to continue your healing.

My Womb Vitality Self Study modules are designed to accompany you on your womb healing journey, bringing you extra confidence and clarity to achieve your goals.

In these modules I guide you to fully heal, layer by layer, so that you get to dig deeply and release at all levels. Undergo profound releases as you discover and root out blockages at all chakra levels.

You've already felt shifts from connecting with your blockages and just know that by digging deeper you will be experiencing more powerful releases. Let's get your quality of life back as you dedicate time to transforming your heavy energies into confidence and flow.

The modules are perfectly structured and timed to fit into your schedule so that you can easily fit in a womb connection session every day. It is also available as an App.

Follow the link or scan the QR code:

https://wombhealing.ohmymamabody.com/5stepstechnique-selfstudymodules

Work With Vicki 1:1

If you feel you just would like that 1:1 guidance to achieve fast and long lasting healing, I invite you to apply for a call with me. Let's discuss which support is best aligned with where you are currently at so that you get the most out of your 1:1 healing journey.

Follow the link or scan the QR code:

https://wombhealing.ohmymamabody.com/5stepstechnique-bonuses

CHAPTER FIFTEEN

ABOUT THE AUTHOR

Vicki Renz started Oh My Mama Body in 2019 with the intention to reach and support women to understand their bodies during their fertility journey. Everything Vicki does is based on her own experiences of recurrent miscarriage, unexplained infertility and healing.

Thanks to an online educational company, Vicki was able to learn the technical skills to create her website, YouTube channel, courses, and the marketing skills to create her emails and help women to find her much-needed guidance.

Do you also have a passion (or would love to find your calling) you would like to share with the world and don't know where to start? Well, you definitely can, so follow your heart and share your message with the world. Here are some free videos to get you started:

https://tinyurl.com/learnskillslikevicki

Vicki reaches hundreds of thousands of women daily with her relatable and supportive content on social media.

She absolutely loves supporting women in her Tribe and 1:1, it's such a joy for her to witness so many beautiful transformations as ladies discover womb healing for themselves.

When she is not working with the energies, Vicki enjoys traveling and adventure from camping in the French Alps to diving in the south Pacific.

Above all, Vicki loves spending time with her family; supporting and motivating her sons with their hobbies and passions.

All enquiries for podcast appearances, video shows and speaking can be sent to vicki@ohmymamabody.com

Follow Vicki on social media (click on the icon or scan the QR code):

VICKI_OHMYMAMABODY YouTube

Printed in Poland
by Amazon Fulfillment
Poland Sp. z o.o., Wrocław

34259659R00077